EASIEST 5-FINGER PIANO COLLECTION

Top Chart Hits

15 popular chart hits arranged for 5-finger piano

Wise Publications
part of The Music Sales Group
London / New York / Paris / Sydney / Copenhagen / Berlin / Madrid / Tokyo

CLOWN (Emeli Sandé)

Words & Music by Shahid Khan, Emeli Sandé & Grant Mitchell

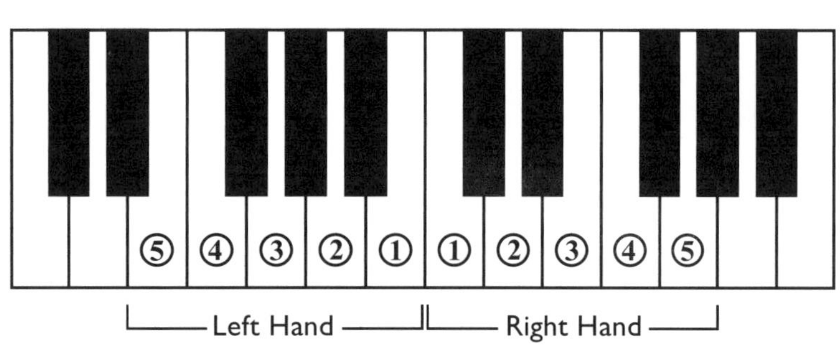

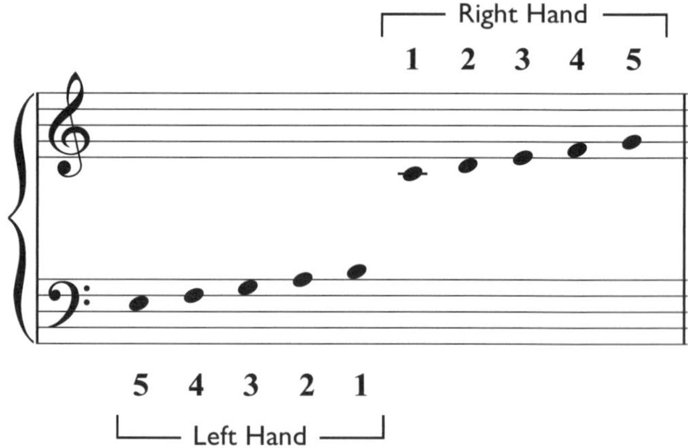

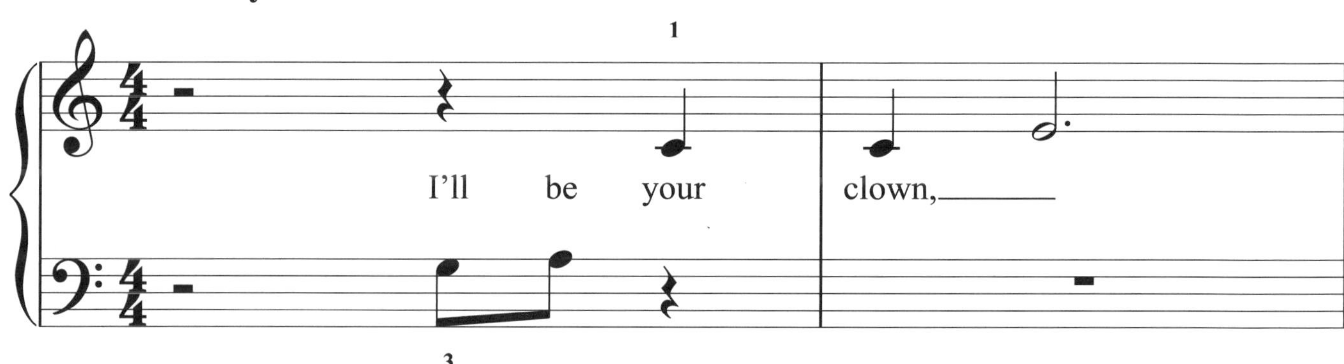

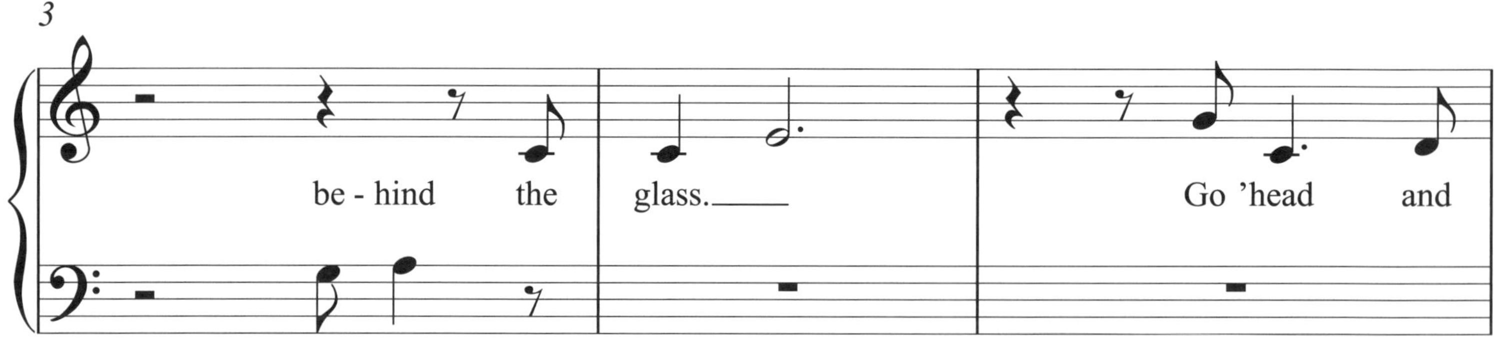

8
too if I saw me. I'll be your clown,
3

11
on your fav - 'rite chan - nel.

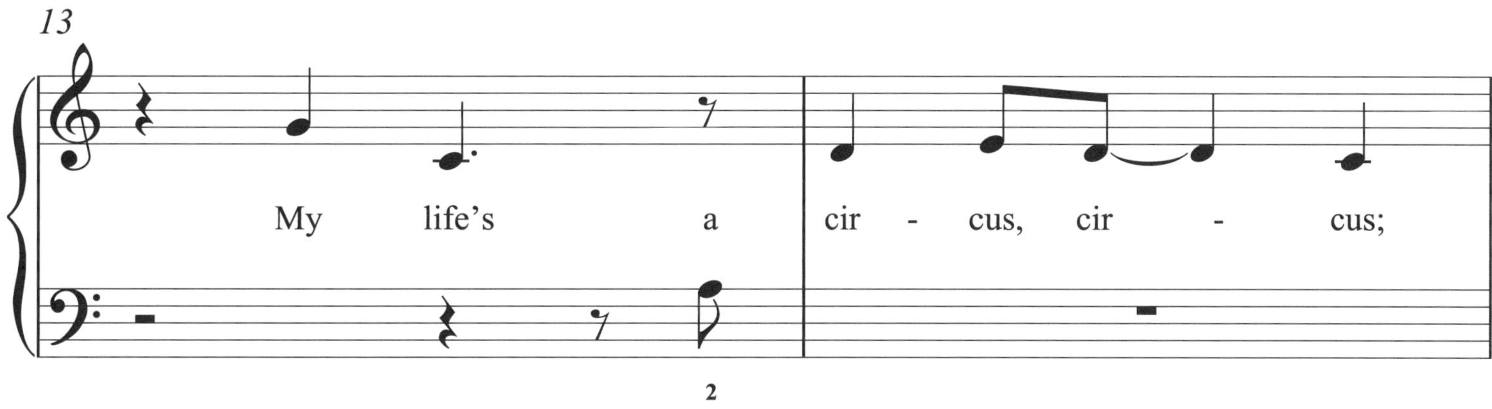
13
My life's a cir - cus, cir - cus;
2

15
round in cir - cles, sell - ing out to - night.

I KNEW YOU WERE TROUBLE (Taylor Swift)

Words & Music by Max Martin, Taylor Swift & Shellback

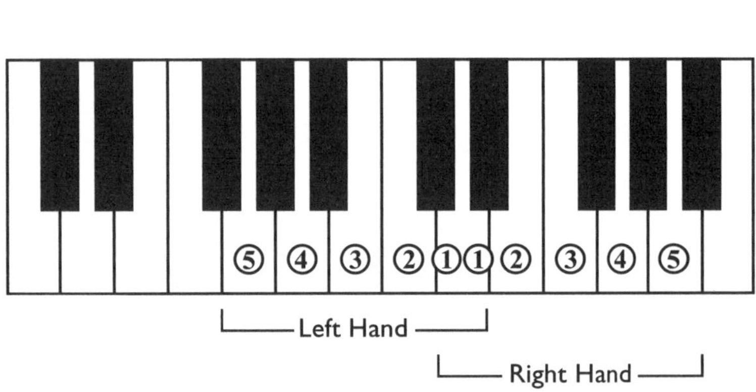

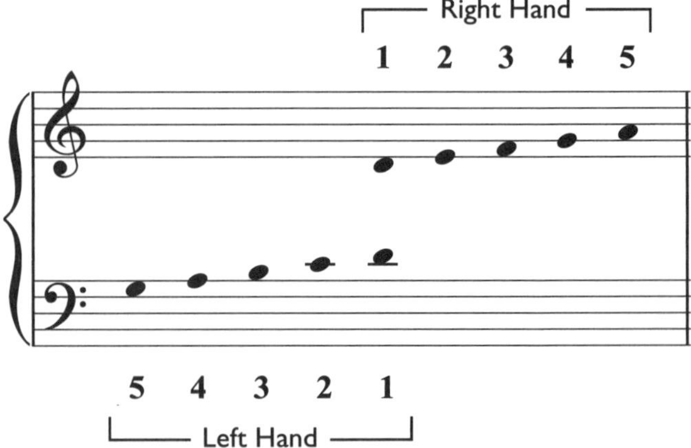

8
1.
2
2.
till you put me down. Oh,
now I'm

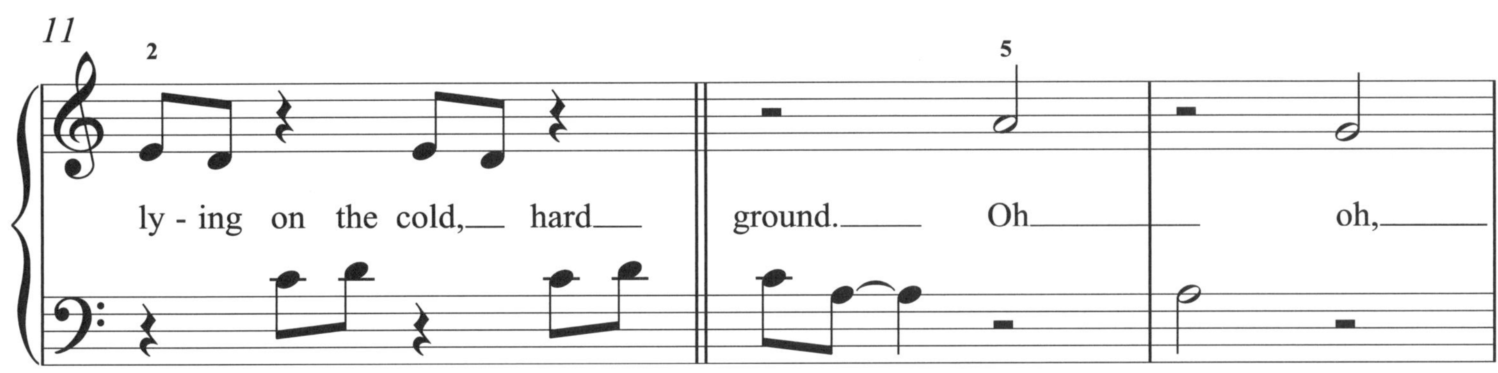
11
2
5
ly - ing on the cold, hard
ground. Oh
oh,

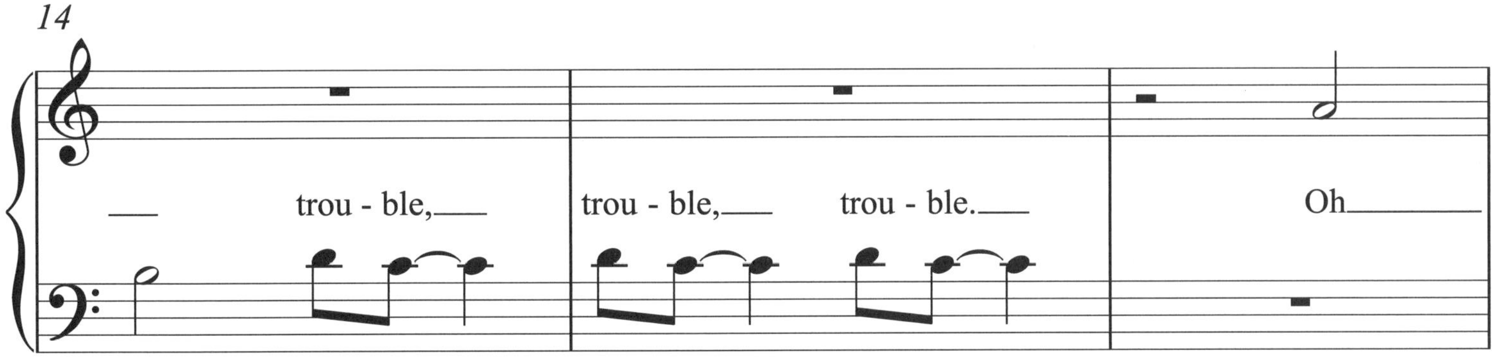
14
trou - ble,
trou - ble, trou - ble.
Oh

17
oh,
trou - ble,
trou - ble, trou - ble.

RIGHT PLACE RIGHT TIME (Olly Murs)

Words & Music by Stephen Robson, Claude Kelly & Oliver Murs

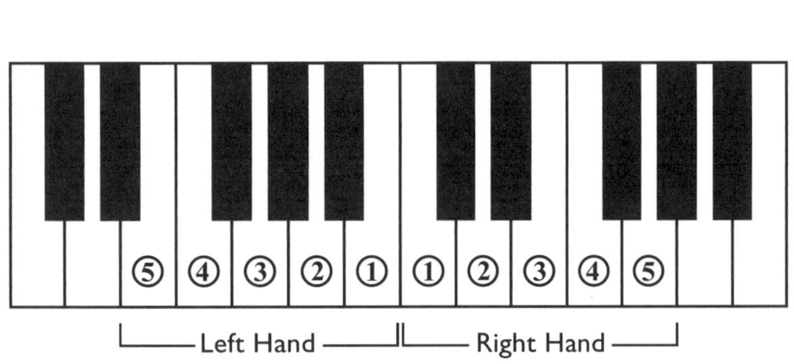

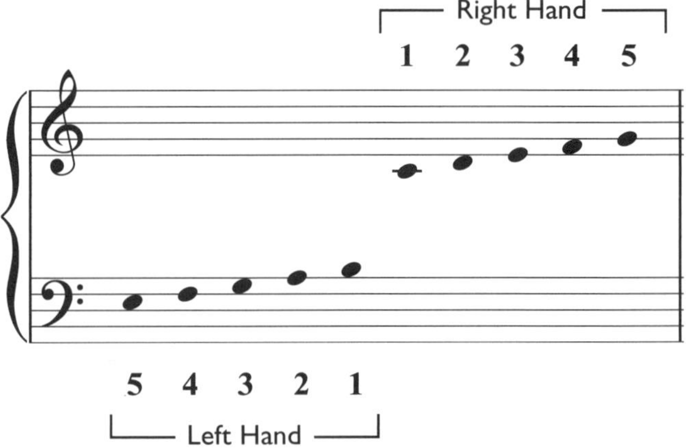

With a driving beat ♩ = 126

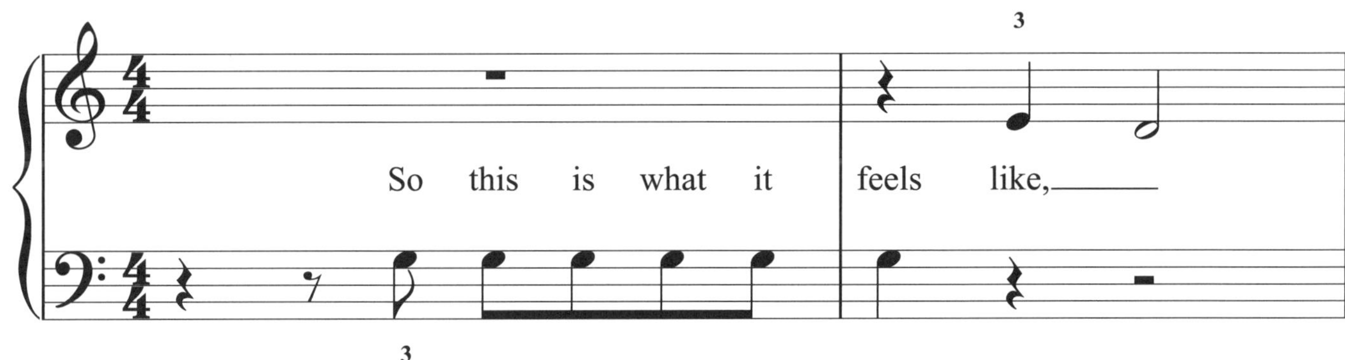

9
3
This is why we came, yeah, I can feel it in my
3
12
veins. Hey, yeah. So this is what it feels like,
15
5
right place, the right time with you.
18
1.
The right place, the right time. Oh,
21
2.
the right place, the right time.

BRAND NEW DAY (Kodaline)

Words & Music by Mark Prendergast, Vincent May & Stephen Garrigan

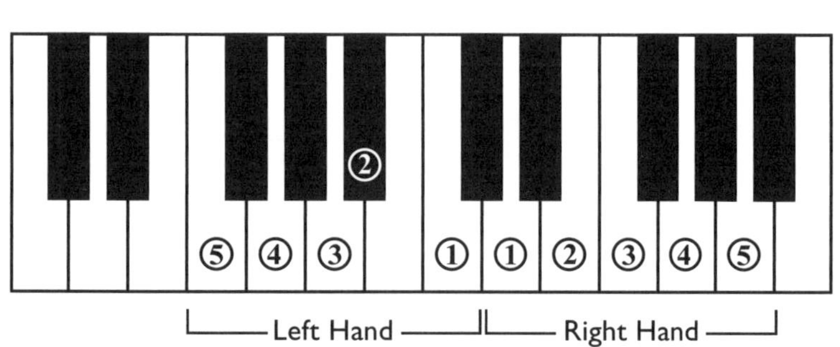

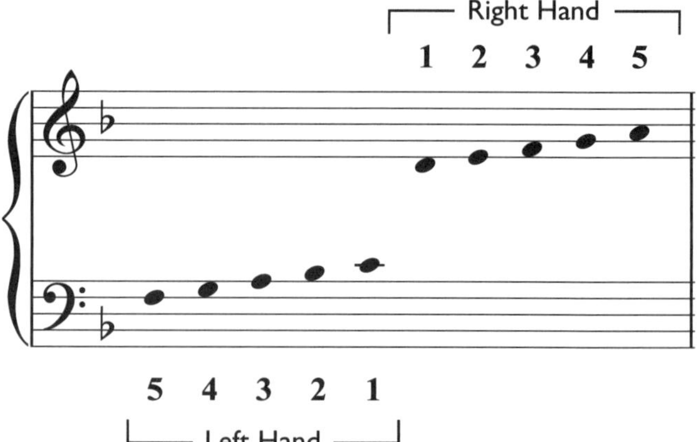

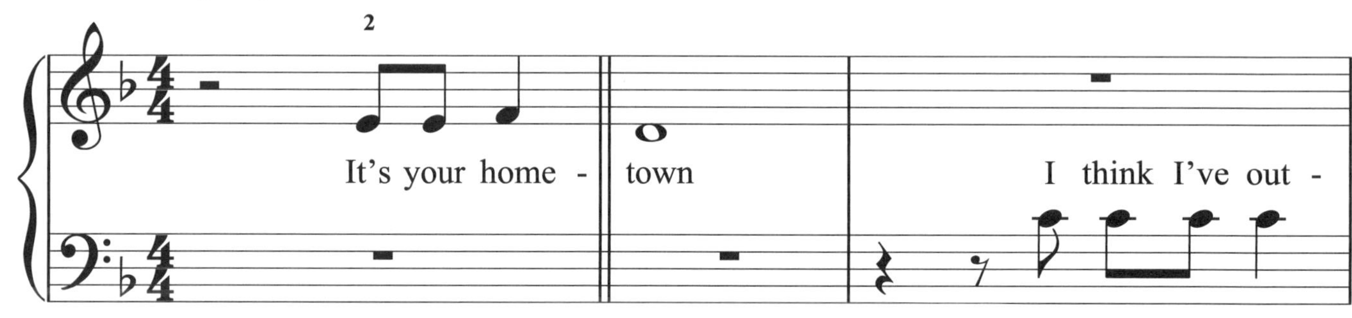

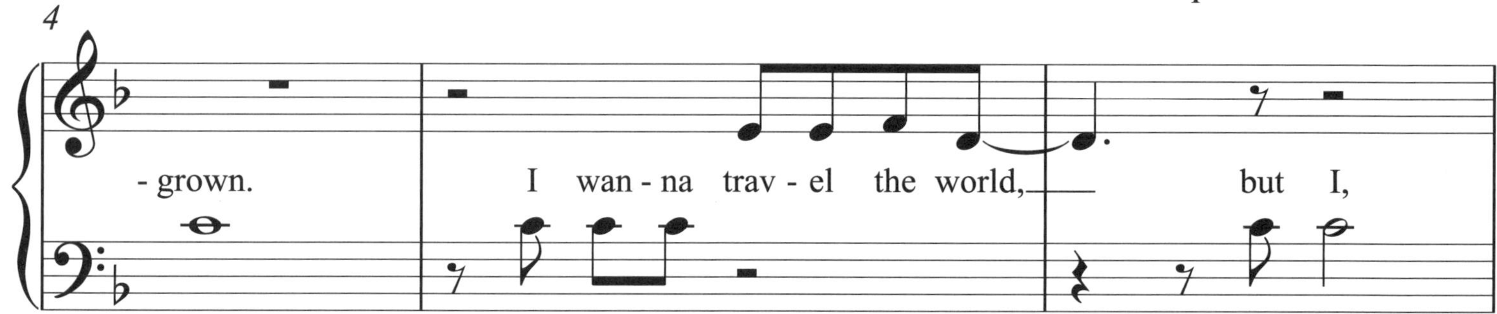

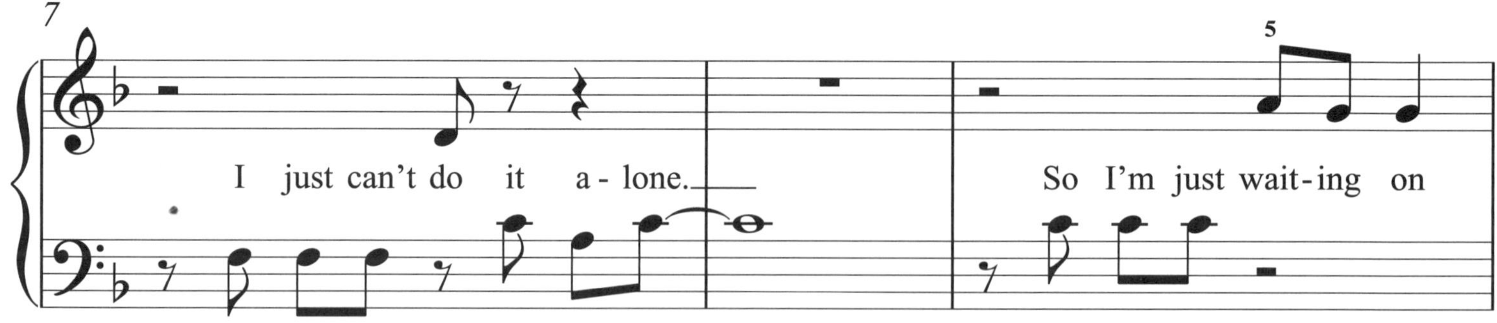

13
2
Think a-bout all the for - eign pla - ces we could be.
1
17
I'll be flick - ing stones at your win - dow, I'll be wait -
20
- ing out - side till you're read - y to go. Won't
22
you come down, come a - way with me? Just think of all the pla - ces
25
we could be. I'll be wait - ing, wait - ing on a brand new day.

WALKS LIKE RIHANNA (The Wanted)

Words & Music by Andrew Hill, Lukasz Gottwald, Henry Russell Walter, Edvard Erfjord & Henrik Michelsen

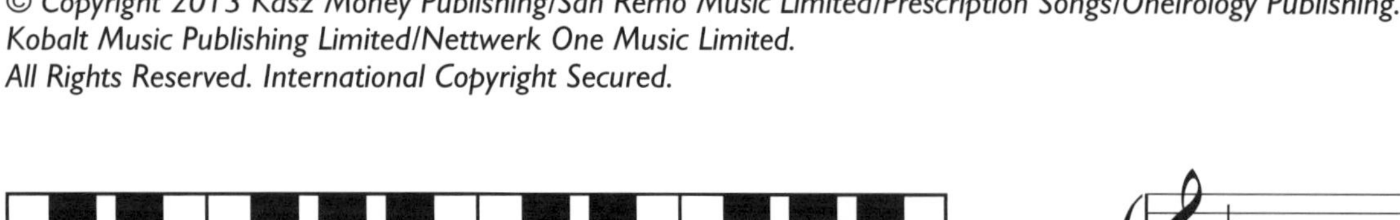

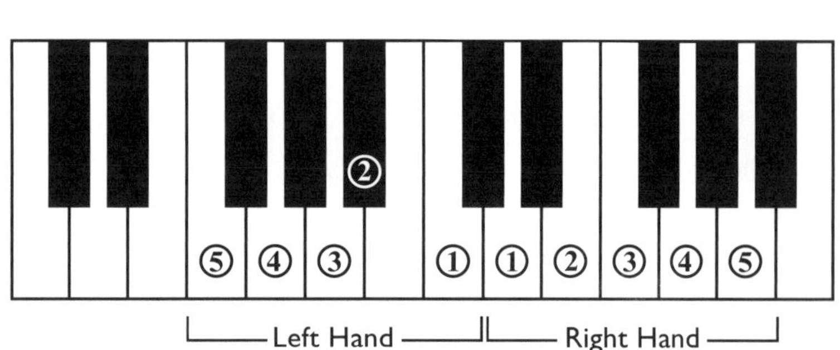

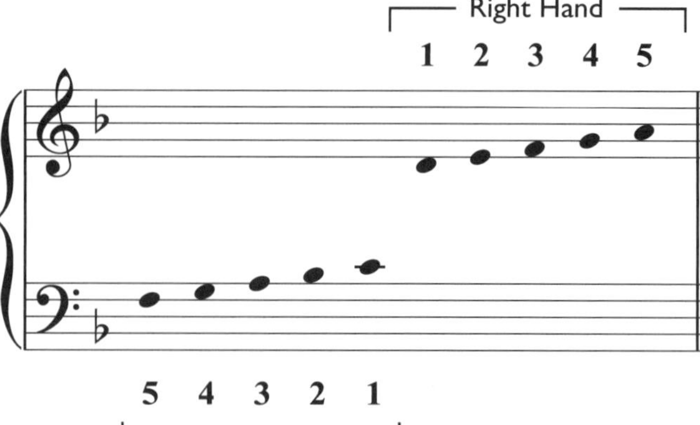

Gracefully ♩ = 112

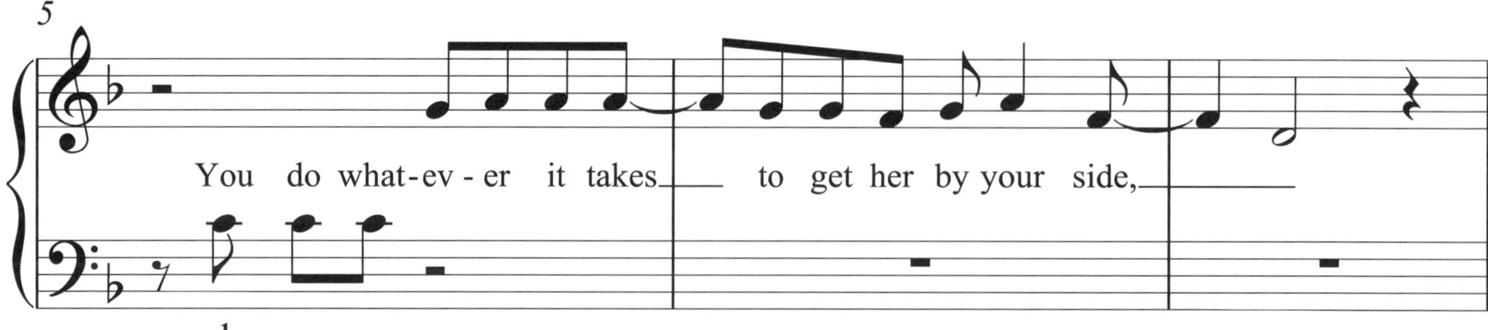

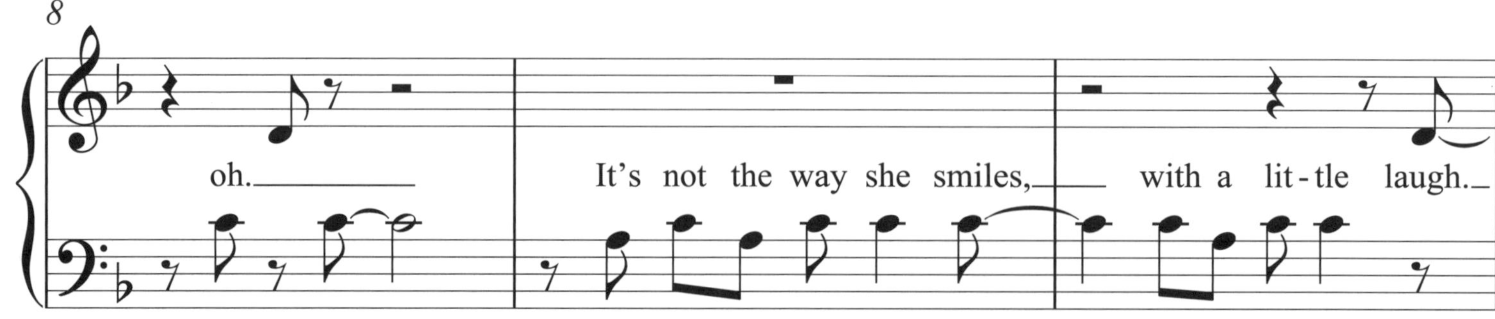

11
It's not the way she looks in a pho - to - graph.
3
13
But all the boys, they crowd a - round.
1
She
17
5
can't sing, she can't dance, but who cares? She
20
walks like Ri - han - na. She can't sing, she can't dance, but
23
1.
2.
who cares? She walks like Ri - han - na. She walks like Ri - han - na.

ROAR (Katy Perry)

Words & Music by Lukasz Gottwald, Bonnie McKee, Katy Perry, Martin Max & Henry Russell Walter

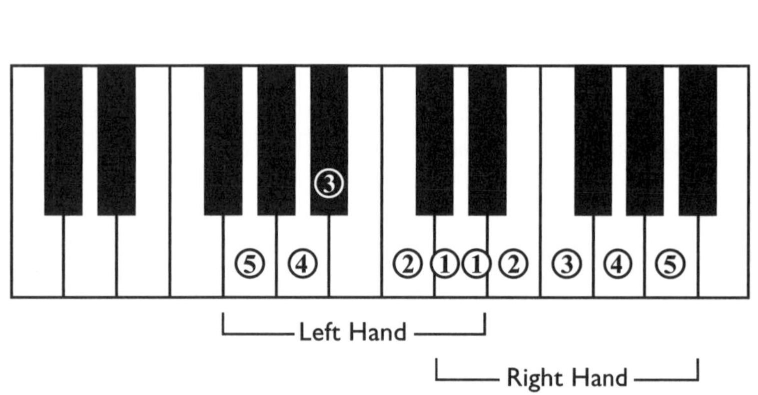

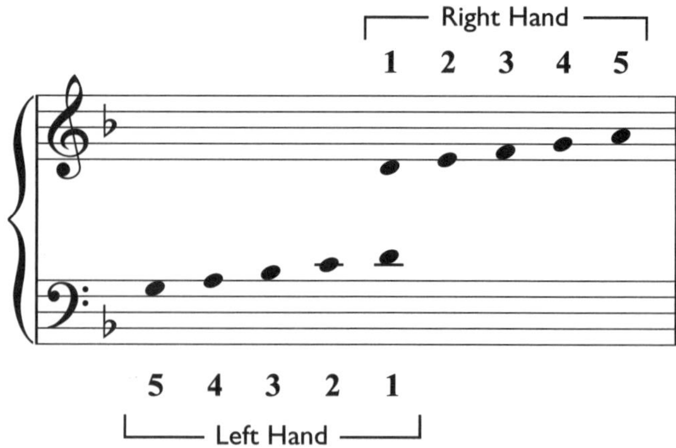

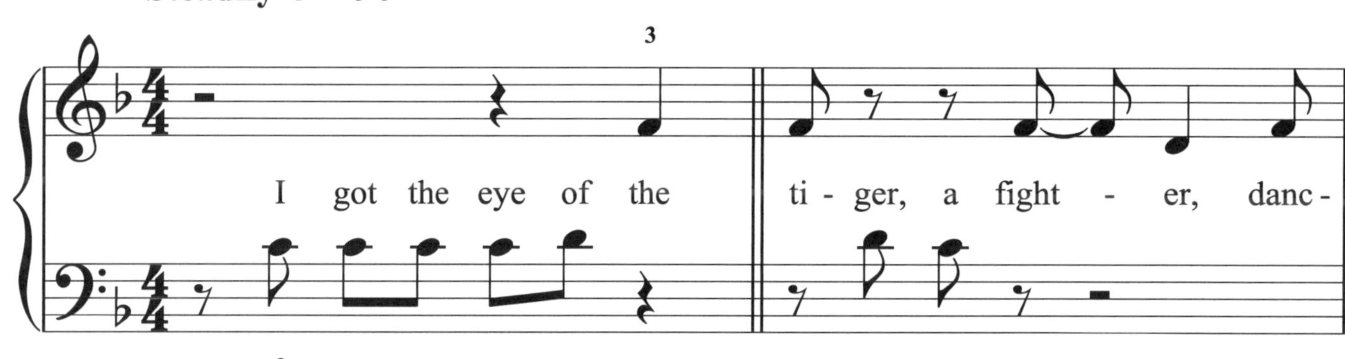

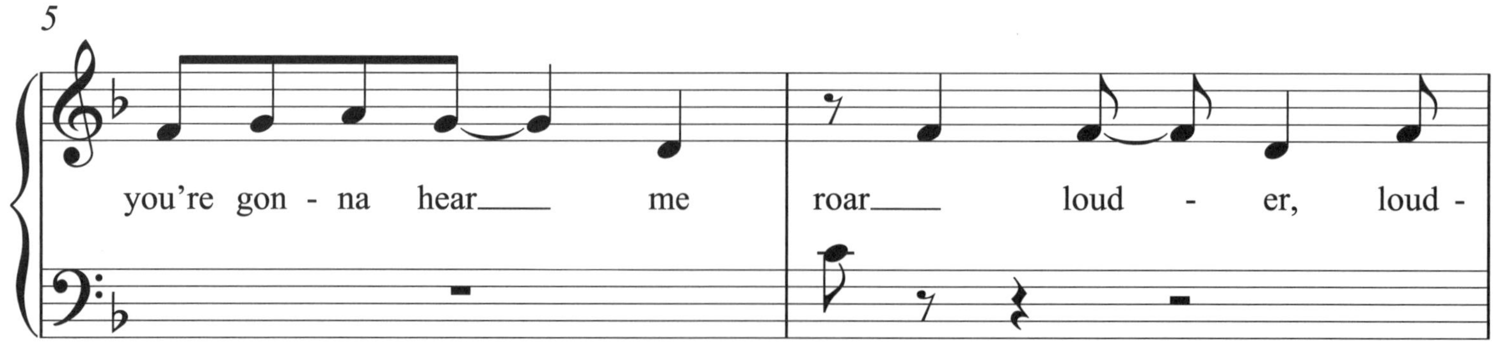

7
-der than a li - on, 'cause
I am a cham - pion, and

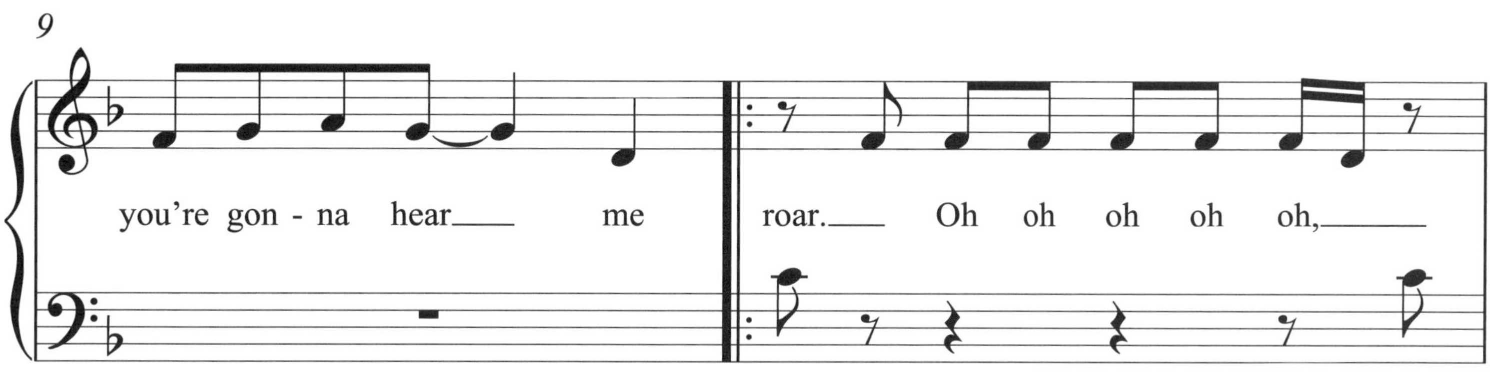
9
you're gon - na hear___ me
roar.___ Oh oh oh oh oh,___

11
oh___ oh oh oh oh oh.___
Oh___ oh oh oh oh oh,___

13
you're gon - na hear___ me
roar.___

WHAT ABOUT US (The Saturdays feat. Sean Paul)

Words & Music by Oliver Jacobs, Phillip Jacobs, Sean Henriques & Camille Purcell

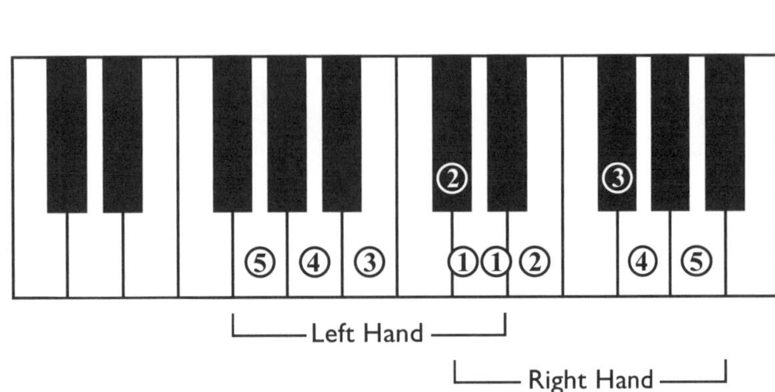

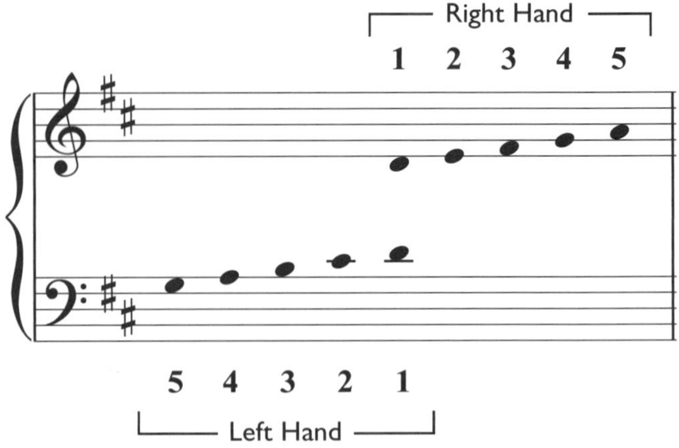

Rhythmically ♩ = 108

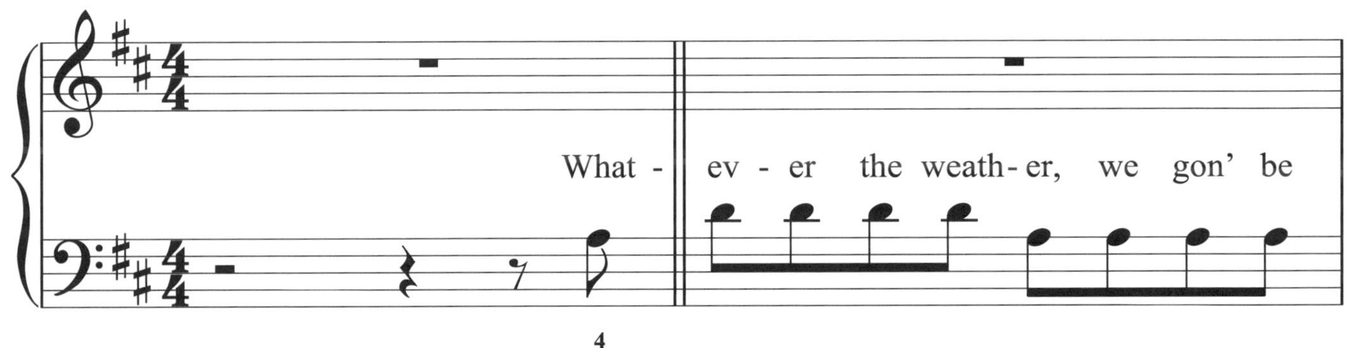

7
2
give in and take it? So what's up ba - by? What a - bout
9
us? What ya do - in' to my head?
11
Should be here with me in - stead.
13
What a - bout those words you said? What a - bout
1
16
us? What a - bout us?

BEST SONG EVER (One Direction)

Words & Music by Wayne Hector, John Ryan, Julian Bunetta & Edward Drewett

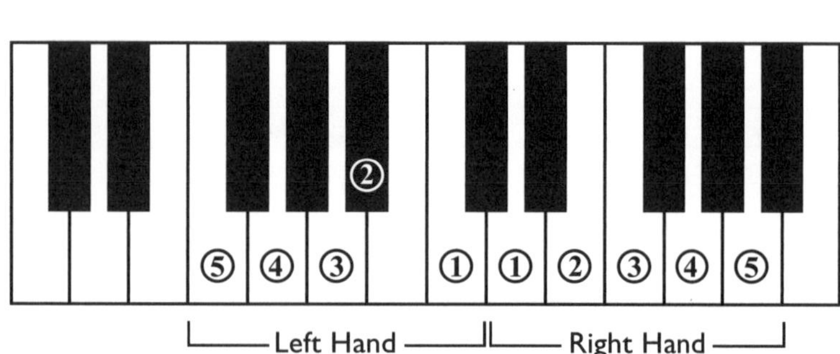

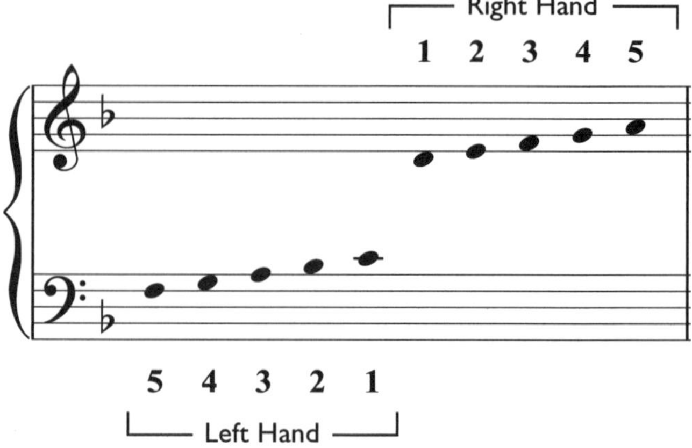

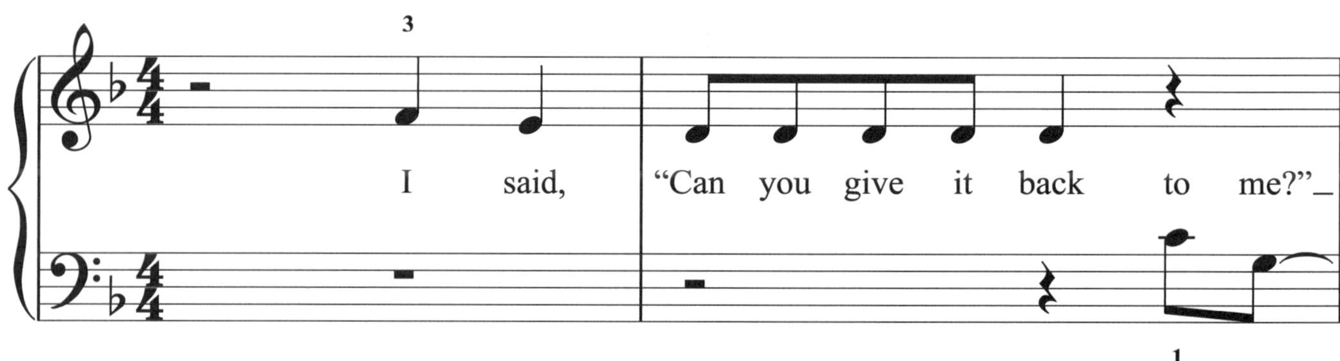

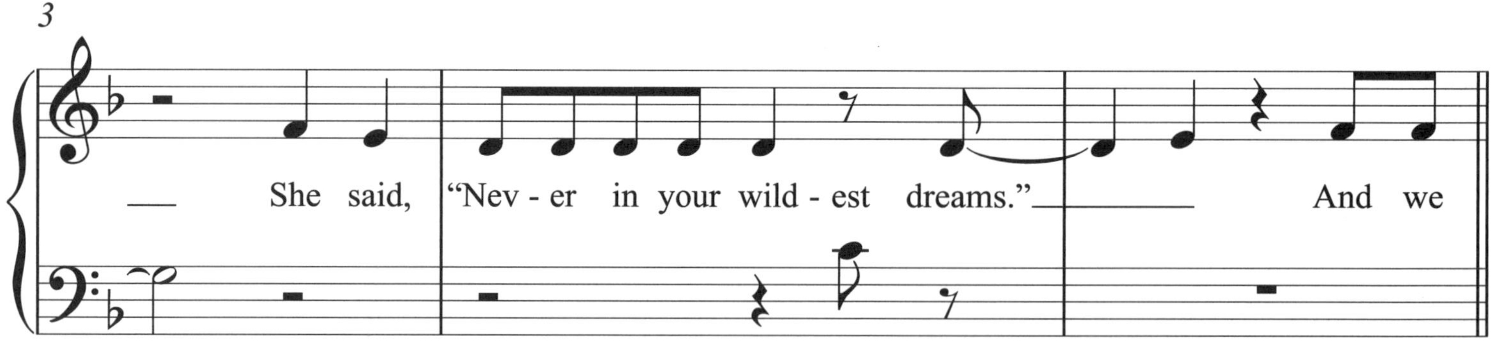

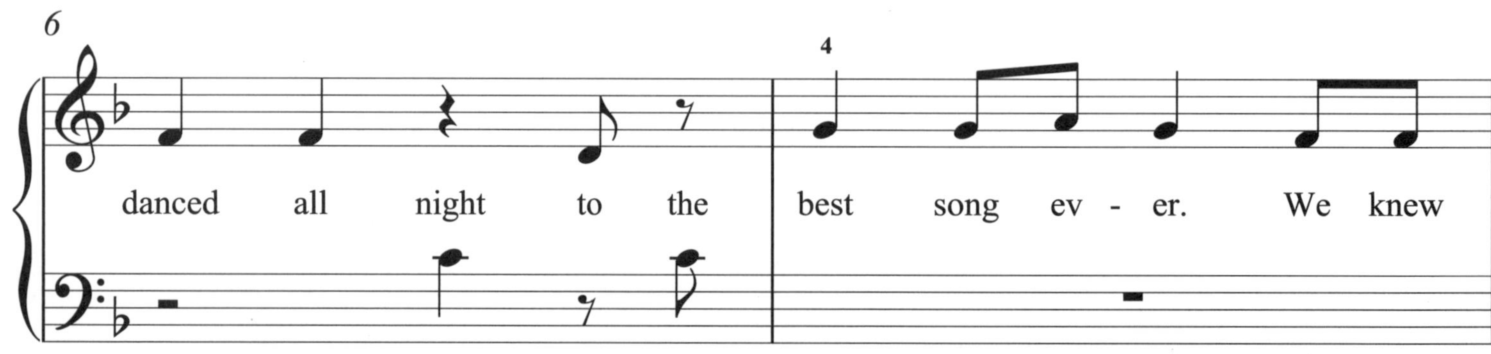

8
ev - 'ry line; now I
can't re-mem-ber how it
goes, but I know that I
1

11
won't for - get her 'cause we
danced all night to the

13
best song ev - er. I think it went
oh oh___ oh,___ I think it went
5

15
1
5
3
4
2
yeah yeah___ yeah,___ I think it goes...___
whoa!
2
5

LET HER GO (Passenger)

Words & Music by Michael Rosenberg

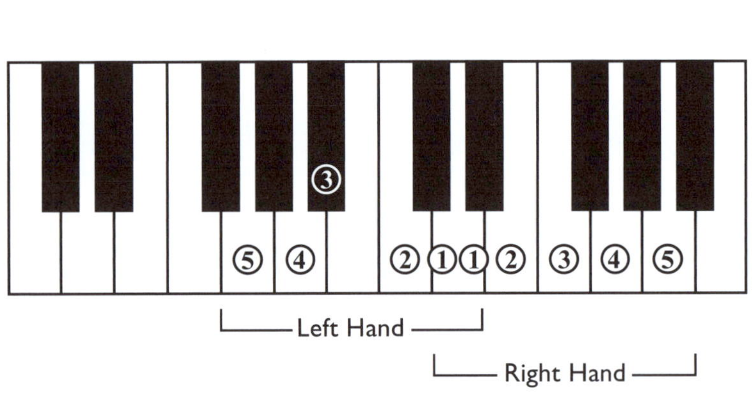

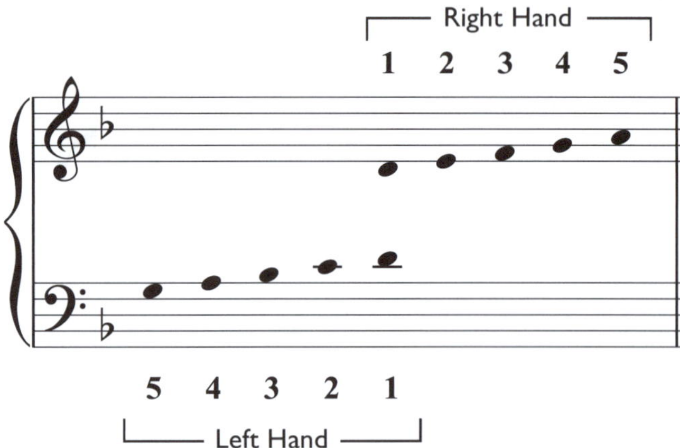

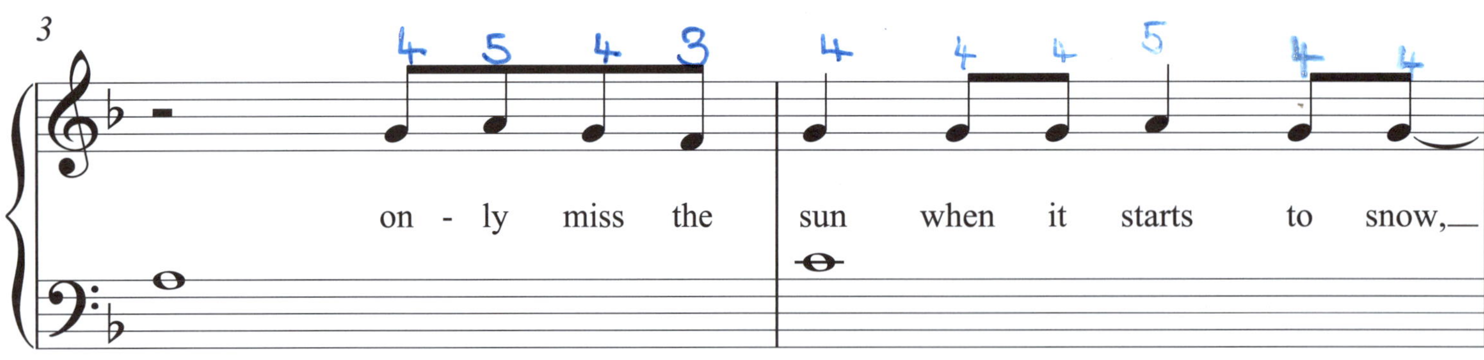

8
5
On - ly know you've been
10
high when you're feel - ing low,
on - ly hate the
12
road when you're miss - ing home,
on - ly know you
14
love her when you let her go;
16
and you let her go.

PANIC CORD (Gabrielle Aplin)

Words & Music by Jez Ashurst, Gabrielle Aplin & Nicholas Atkinson

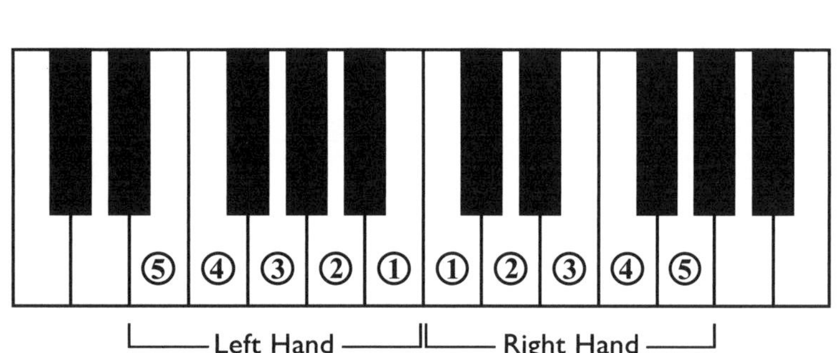

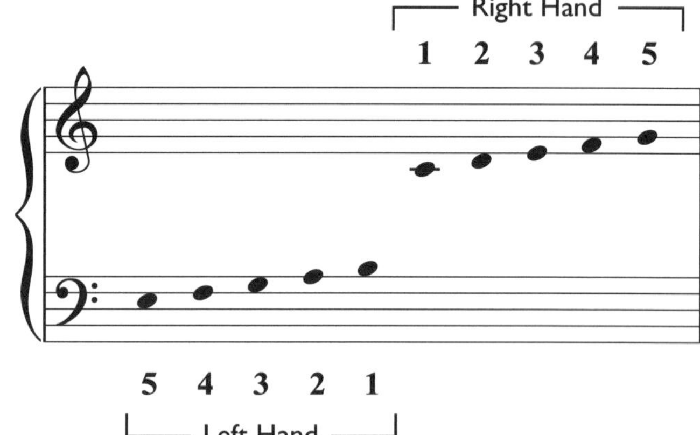

Lightly, with a bounce ♩ = 104

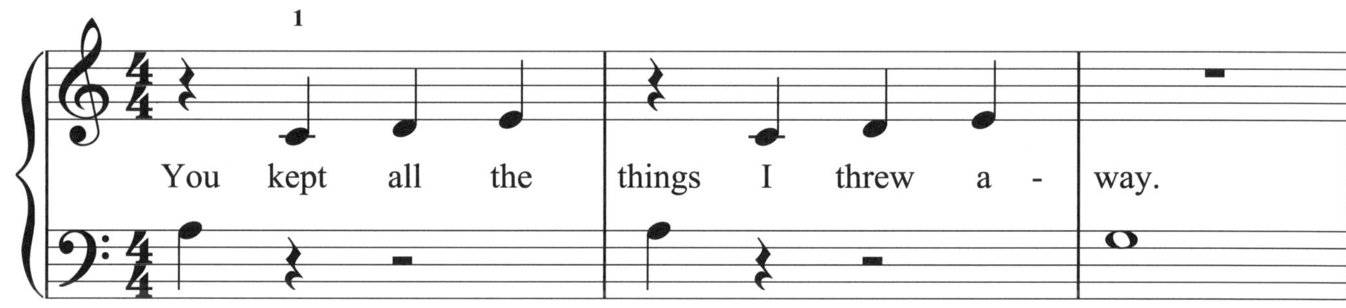

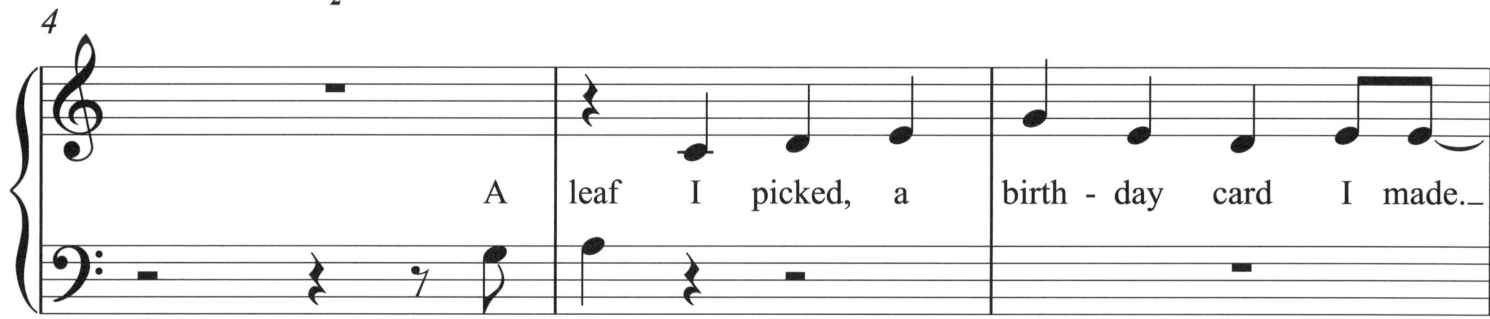

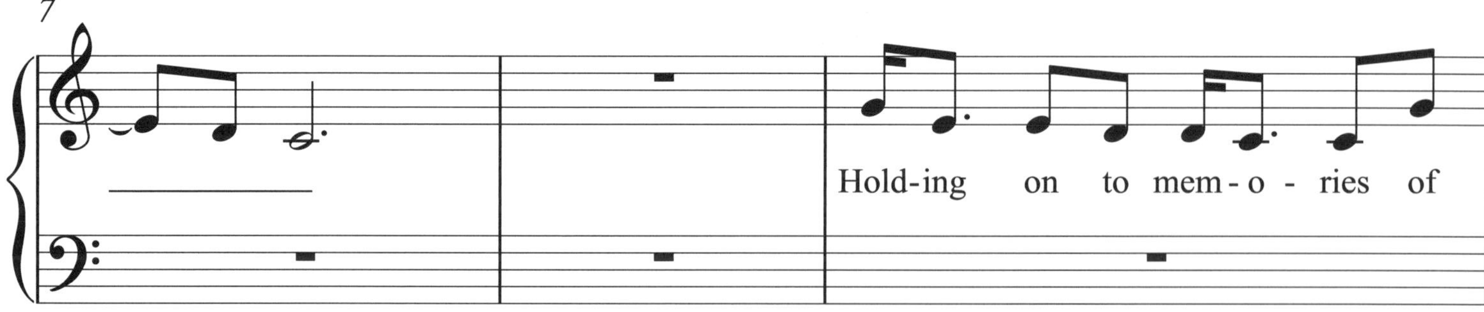

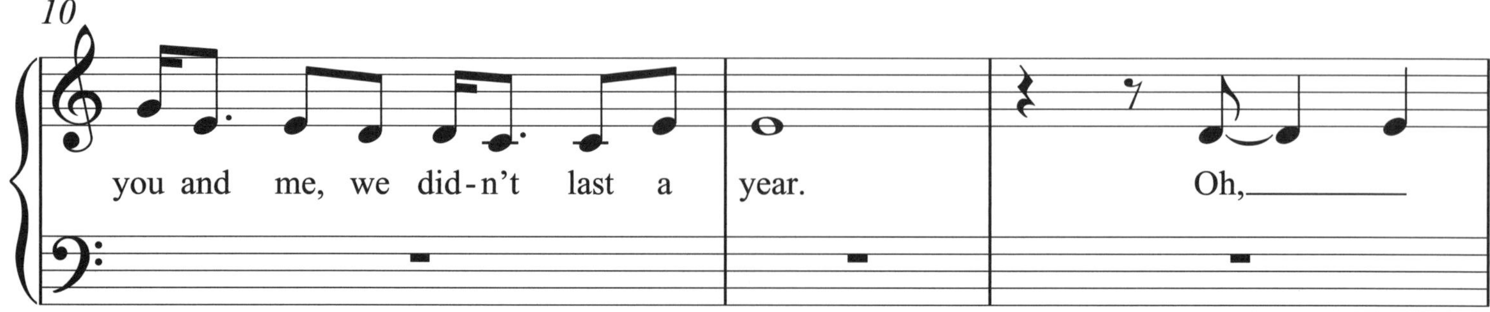

13
we're just a box of sou - ven - irs.
'Cause
2
15
may - be
I pulled the pan - ic
cord, and may - be
18
you were hap - py, I was
bored. May - be I want - ed you to
20
change;
may - be I'm the one to
22
blame,
may - be I'm the one to
blame.

POMPEII (Bastille)

Words & Music by Daniel Campbell Smith

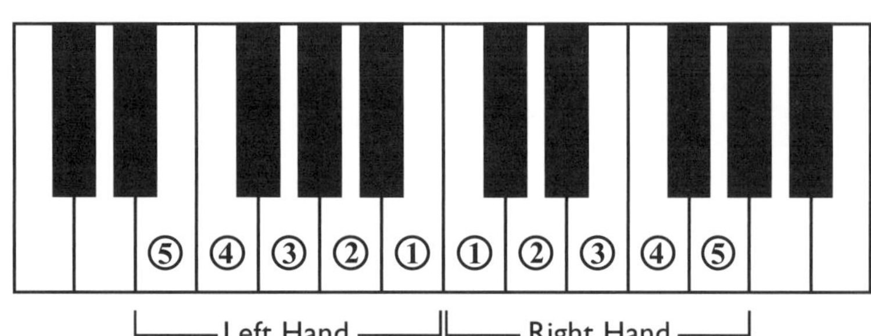

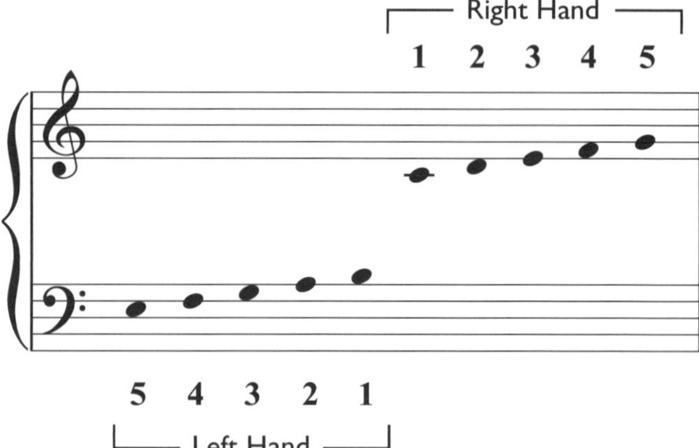

Smoothly ♩ = 100

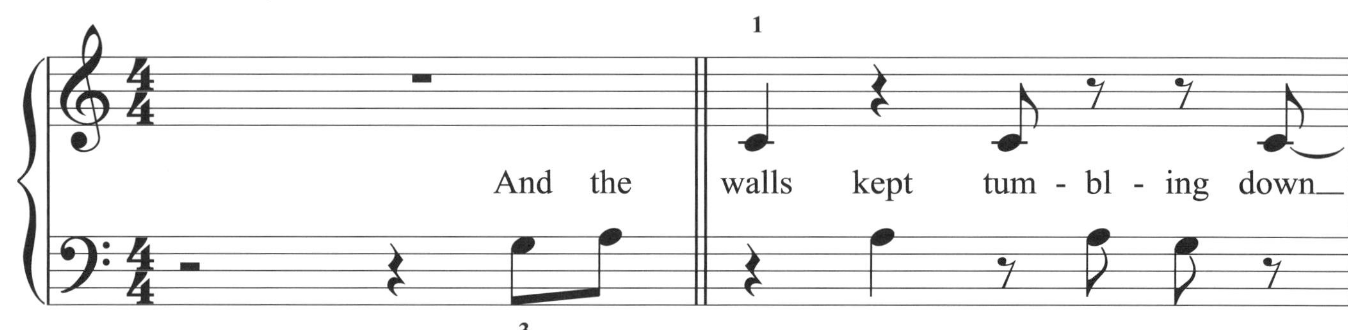

12
- most feel like noth - ing changed at all? And if you close your eyes,
15
does it al - most feel like you've been here be-fore?
2
4
18
How am I gon-na be an op-ti-mist a - bout this? How
2
4
3
5
1
3
21
am I gon-na be an op-ti-mist a - bout this?
Eh-oh eh-oh, eh,
2
4
3
5
1
3
24
eh-oh eh-oh, eh, eh-oh eh-oh, eh, eh-oh eh-oh.
1
3

DEAR DARLIN' (Olly Murs)

Words & Music by James Eliot, Edward Drewett & Oliver Murs

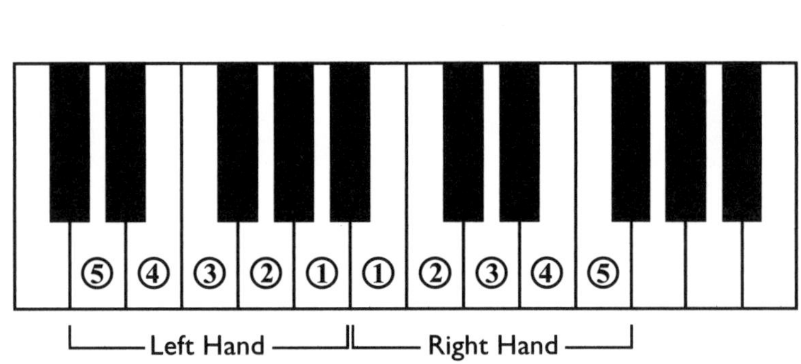

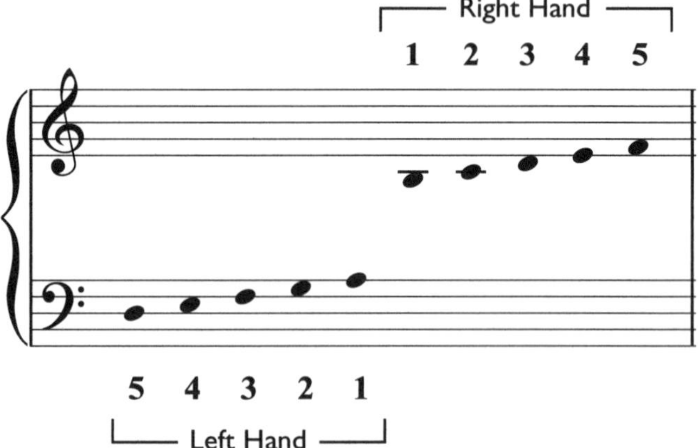

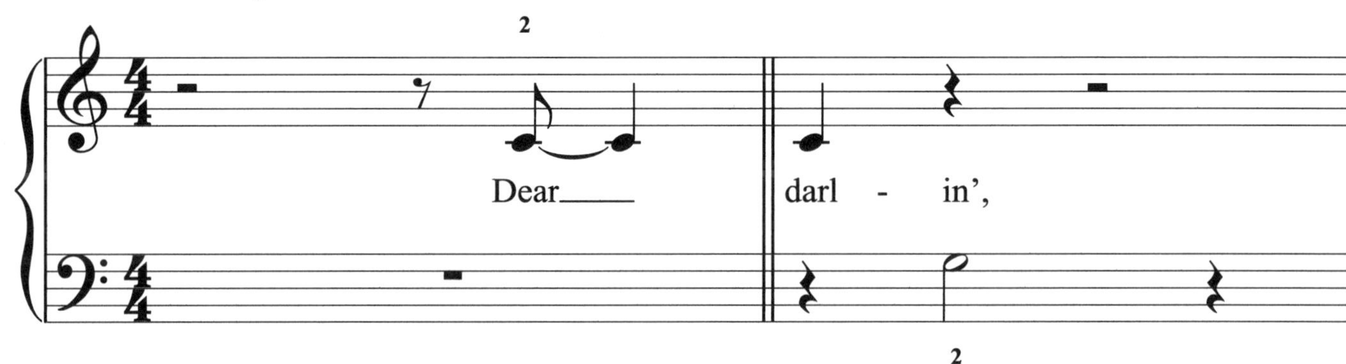

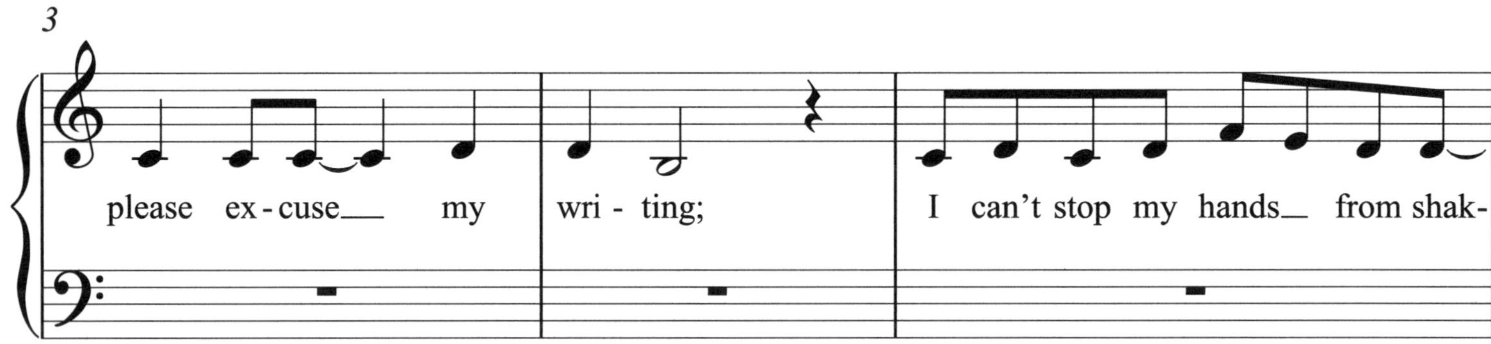

8
I miss you, and
1
3

11
noth - ing hurts like no you, and
2
4

13
no one un - der - stands what we went through; it was
1
4

15
short, it was sweet, we tried. We tried.
1
3
2
4

BURN (Ellie Goulding)

Words & Music by Greg Kurstin, Ryan Tedder, Brent Kutzle, Noel Zancanella & Elena Goulding

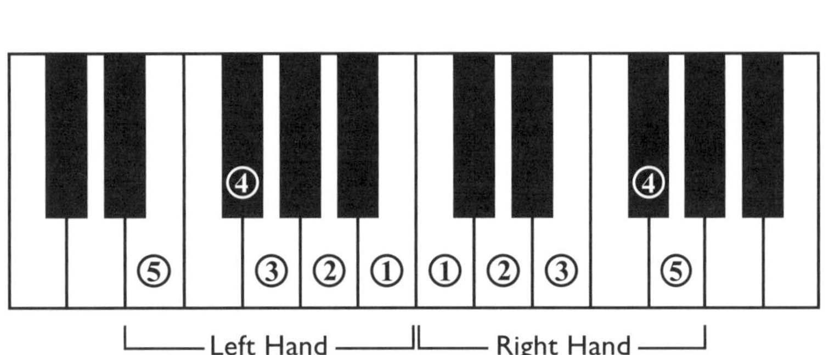

13
'Cause we got the fire, fire, fire. Yeah, we got the
16
fire, fire, fire, and we're gon-na let it burn, burn, burn,
19
burn. We're gon-na let it burn, burn, burn, burn. Gon-na let it
22
burn, burn, burn, burn. We're gon - na let it
24
burn, burn, burn. And we're gon - na let it burn.

FLATLINE (Mutya Keisha Siobhan)

Words & Music by Keisha Buchanan, Mutya Buena, Siobhan Donaghy & Devon Hynes

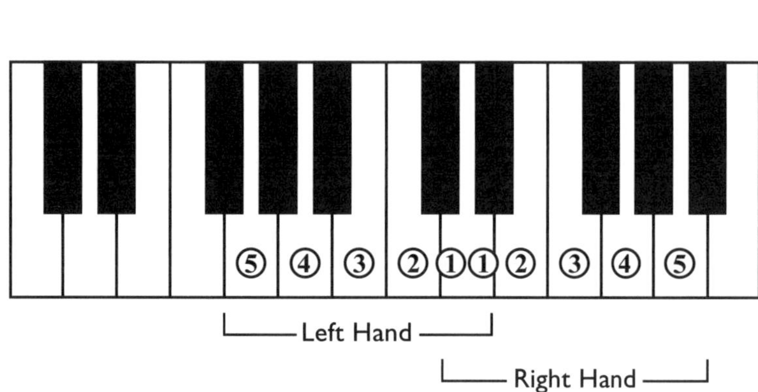

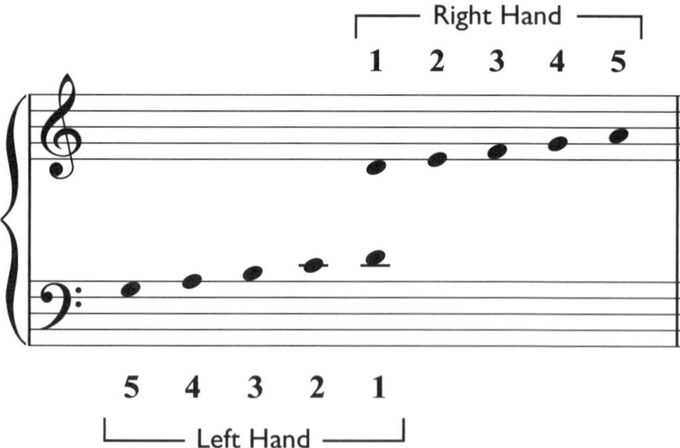

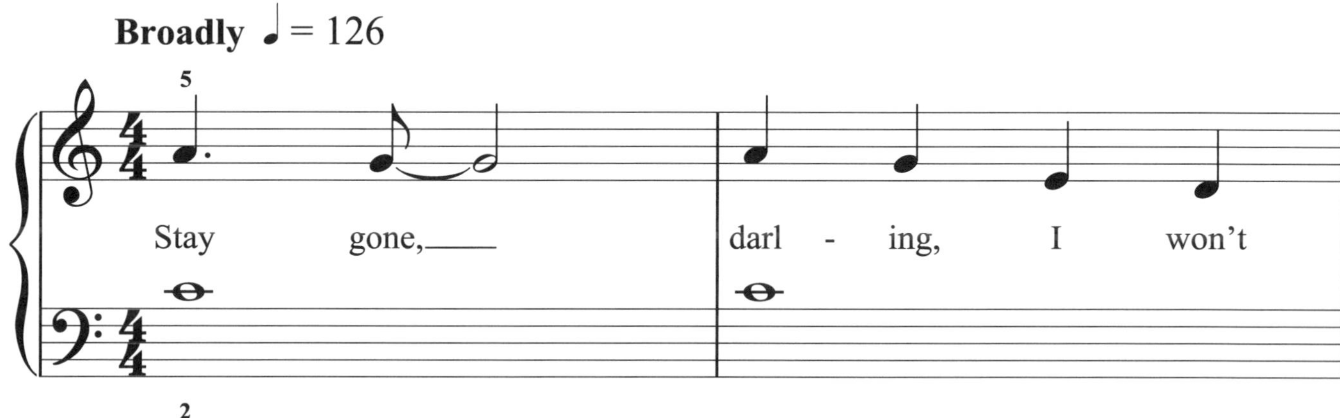

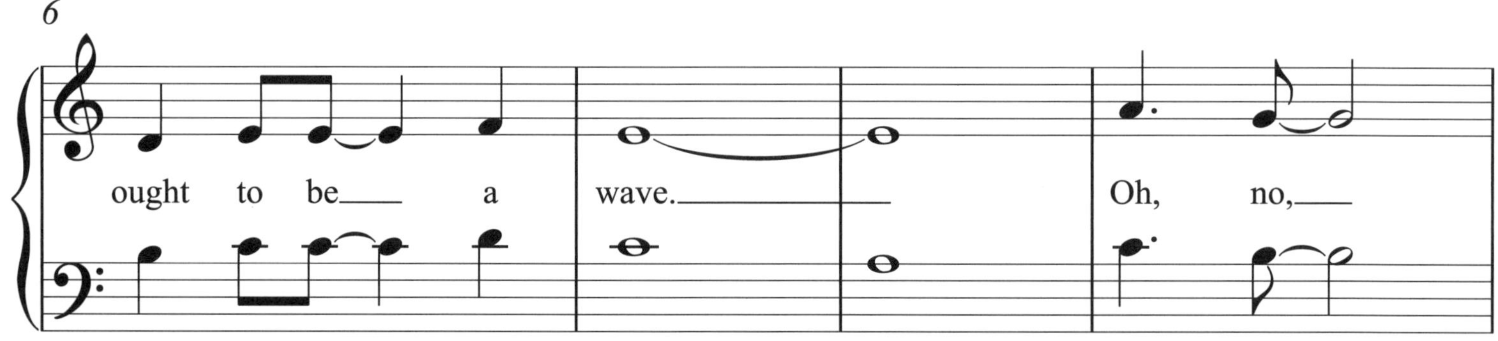

10
darl - ing, I can't hang on; I can feel a
13
flat - line that ought to be a wave.
16
Oh oh
2
4
19
oh oh oh.
Oh oh
3
5
2
5
22
oh oh oh.
2
4

JUST GIVE ME A REASON (Pink feat. Nate Ruess)

Words & Music by Alecia Moore, Jeff Bhasker & Nate Ruess

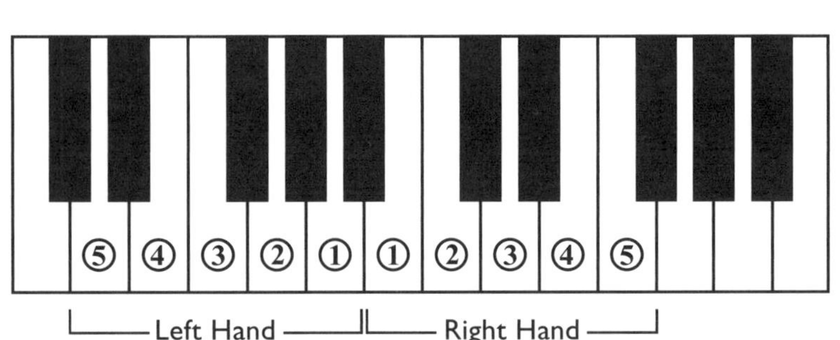

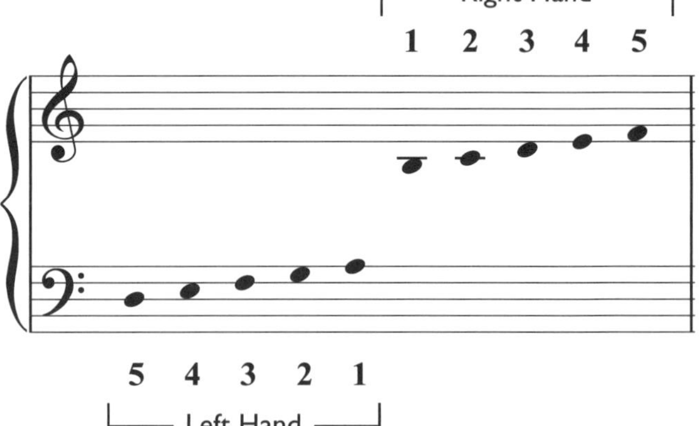

8
5 2
5 1
4
love, our love.
Just give me a rea - son, just a
11
lit - tle bit's e - nough. Just a sec - ond, we're not bro - ken, just bent,
13
and we can learn to love a - gain. It's in the stars, it's been
15
writ - ten in the scars on our hearts: we're not bro - ken, just bent,
17
and we can learn to love a - gain.

2 3 4 5 6 7 8 9

EASIEST 5-FINGER PIANO COLLECTION

ALSO AVAILABLE IN THE SERIES...

Abba
A great collection of 15 classic Abba hits, including 'Dancing Queen', 'Fernando', 'Take A Chance On Me' and 'Thank You For The Music'.
AM998404

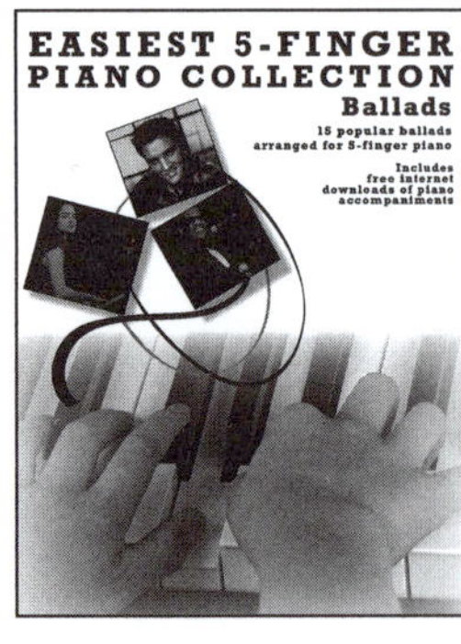

Ballads
A superb collection of 15 well-known ballads, including 'Fix You', 'I Have A Dream', 'Let It Be' and 'What A Wonderful World'.
AM995346

The Beatles
15 classic Beatles hits including 'All My Loving', 'Hey Jude', 'She Loves You' and 'Yellow Submarine'.
NO91322

New Chart Hits
15 top chart hits including 'Cry Me Out', 'Don't Stop Believin'', 'Issues', 'Just Dance' and 'Russian Roulette'.
AM1001077

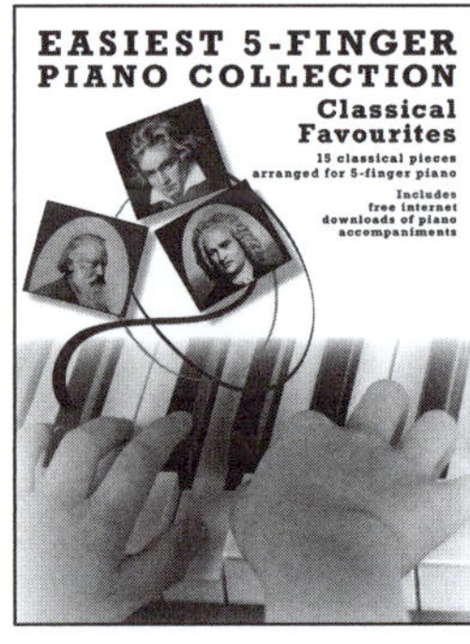

Classical Favourites
15 classical pieces including 'Jupiter' (Holst), 'Lullaby' (Brahms), 'Minuet In G' (J.S. Bach) and 'Spring' (Vivaldi).
AM998393

Film Songs
15 great film songs including 'Breaking Free', 'Don't Worry, Be Happy', 'Somewhere Out There' and 'You've Got A Friend In Me'.
AM995335

Showtunes
15 great showtunes including 'Any Dream Will Do', 'Circle Of Life', 'Mamma Mia' and 'My Favourite Things'.
AM995324

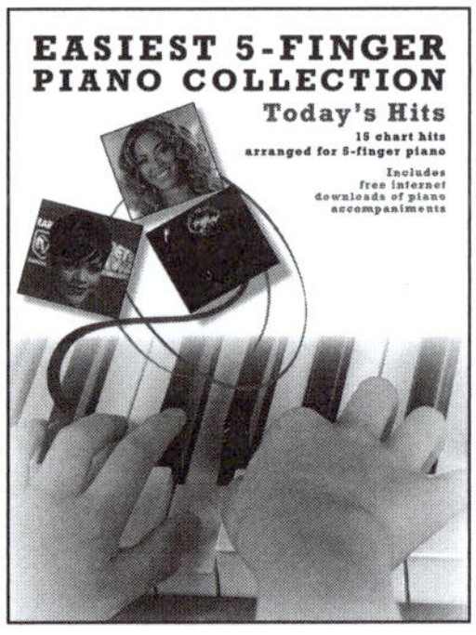

Today's Hits
15 of today's current chart hits including 'Hallelujah', 'Human', 'If I Were A Boy' and 'Viva La Vida'.
AM998415

...PLUS MANY MORE

Download to your computer a set of piano accompaniments for this *Top Chart Hits* edition
(to be played by a teacher/parent).
Visit: **www.hybridpublications.com**
Registration is free and easy.
Your registration code is ON441

Published by
Wise Publications
14-15 Berners Street,
London W1T 3LJ, UK.

Exclusive Distributors:
Music Sales Limited
Distribution Centre, Newmarket Road,
Bury St Edmunds, Suffolk IP33 3YB, UK.
Music Sales Pty Limited
Units 3-4, 17 Willfox Street, Condell Park
NSW 2200, Australia.

Order No. AM1008106
ISBN 978-1-78305-406-0

Edited by Jenni Norey.
Arranged by Chris Hussey.
Music processed by Camden Music Services.

Printed in the EU.

Your Guarantee of Quality
As publishers, we strive to produce every book to the highest commercial standards. This book has been carefully designed to minimise awkward page turns and to make playing from it a real pleasure. Particular care has been given to specifying acid-free, neutral-sized paper made from pulps which have not been elemental chlorine bleached. This pulp is from farmed sustainable forests and was produced with special regard for the environment. Throughout, the printing and binding have been planned to ensure a sturdy, attractive publication which should give years of enjoyment. If your copy fails to meet our high standards, please inform us and we will gladly replace it.

www.musicsales.com